Leading the Way with GPS

by Jack L. Roberts

TABLE OF CONTENTS

Model the Standard 2
TEXT 1 GPS: Guiding the World 4
TEXT 2 A Tool for Everyone 14
Glossary/Index 23
Answer Text Evidence Questions 24
Write to Sources .... Inside Back Cover

HOW TO READ THIS BOOK

1. Read the model lesson on pages 2–3.
2. Practice with the questions in the first text.
3. Apply the standard in the other text.
4. Answer the text evidence questions on page 24.

MODEL THE STANDARD

You will learn how to:

Explain Events and Ideas in a Text

Strong readers are able to explain how and why an event or idea in a text is important. They use specific information in the text to support their explanations.

To identify important events and ideas, ask: What happened? Then look for details that answer the question. To explain an event or idea, ask: Why did it happen? Then look for details that explain why it happened.

See how one reader identified important details about events and ideas to answer the questions below.

> **Question 1:** What happened around the year 1050? Which details in the text explain why it happened?
>
> **Answer:** Around 1050, the Chinese developed a magnetic compass. They developed this compass because it was difficult to use the sky to navigate when it was cloudy.
>
> **Question 2:** What happened in the 1400s? Which details in the text explain why it happened?
>
> **Answer:** The Age of Exploration began in the 1400s. The invention of the compass and the wide use of the astrolabe helped usher in the Age of Exploration.

Navigating the Globe

Before the Global Positioning System (GPS) was invented, people used many different ways to navigate their journeys. Thousands of years ago, people used their knowledge of natural patterns in the sky to navigate.

However, often the sky is cloudy and the sun or stars are invisible, making it hard to navigate. Around the year 1050, the Chinese addressed this problem by developing a magnetic compass. With a magnetic compass, a sailor can find north under a cloudy sky.

The next century saw the wide use of a device known as the astrolabe. It is a device used to measure the angle of the sun. Knowing the angle of the sun allowed sailors to calculate their location.

The astrolabe and the compass helped bring about the beginning of the Age of Exploration in the 1400s. Sailors now had the technology to sail around the globe.

For Question 1, the reader identified the event that happened in 1050 as well as details that explain why it happened.

For Question 2, the reader identified an idea that began in the 1400s as well as details that explain why it happened.

Turn the page to begin reading two texts about navigation. As you read, look for details that explain important events and ideas.

GPS: Guiding the World

▲ A GPS satellite orbits the globe twice every twenty-four hours.

A Global Positioning System, or GPS for short, is a tool used for **navigation**. It helps people figure out how to get from one place to another. This **technology** is changing the way we work, communicate, and play.

Thousands of years ago, sailors used **celestial navigation** to figure out where they were going. They studied the sky, with its sun, moon, stars, and planets. These early navigators relied on the rising and setting stars to find their way. Their knowledge was passed from one generation to the next. Celestial navigation is still used today, but in a new way. Today, people still look to the sky, but they are using GPS **satellites** to navigate. As NASA[1] puts it, "Over thirty U.S. navigation satellites are zipping around high above Earth. These satellites can tell us exactly where we are."

Yet, GPS is more than just an easy way to know how to get from one place to another. GPS technology helps rescue workers locate people in distress. It helps scientists predict natural disasters. It even helps people locate the nearest gas station.

1. NASA—National Aeronautics and Space Administration

GPS Basics

GPS is a group of about thirty navigational satellites that orbit Earth twice a day at an altitude of 20,000 kilometers (12,500 miles). As they orbit Earth, they send out radio signals.

A GPS receiver, such as a smartphone, receives these signals and then calculates the distance to the GPS satellite. It does this by figuring how long it took the signals to reach the smartphone.

The smartphone calculates the distance of at least three satellites. It uses that information to calculate its own location on Earth. This process is complicated. But basically the calculation is done using a math concept called trilateration. This has to do with measuring something from three distances.

Once the smartphone knows its location, it can then figure out directions to anywhere—including the nearest pizzeria.

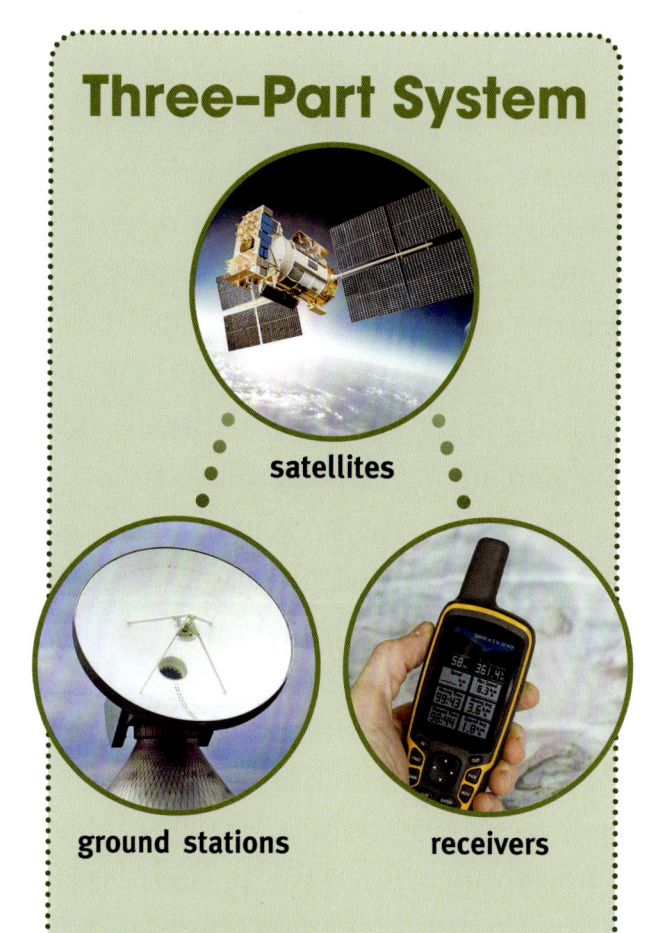

Three-Part System

satellites

ground stations   receivers

GPS SEGMENTS

1. The Space Segment: consists of up to thirty navigation satellites, each in its own orbit; altitude, or height, of orbit is about 20,000 km (12,500 mi) above Earth

2. The User Segment: consists of a receiver, which can be a cell phone, a dashboard device in a car, or a special tracking device; devices receive signals from satellites and then use that information to pinpoint the receiver's exact location on Earth

3. The Control Segment: consists of ground stations; five around the world; make sure the satellites are working properly

GPS: GUIDING THE WORLD

A satellite is an object that **orbits**, or revolves around, a planet or star. For example, Earth is a satellite that orbits the sun. The moon orbits Earth. The moon, Earth, and other planets are natural satellites. But there is another kind of satellite, which is artificial, or human-made. Today, thousands of these satellites orbit Earth. According to NASA, some take pictures of Earth to help weather scientists predict weather. Some take pictures of other planets to help scientists better understand the solar system. Others are used for communication. Finally, there are GPS satellites. These satellites help people navigate around town or around the world.

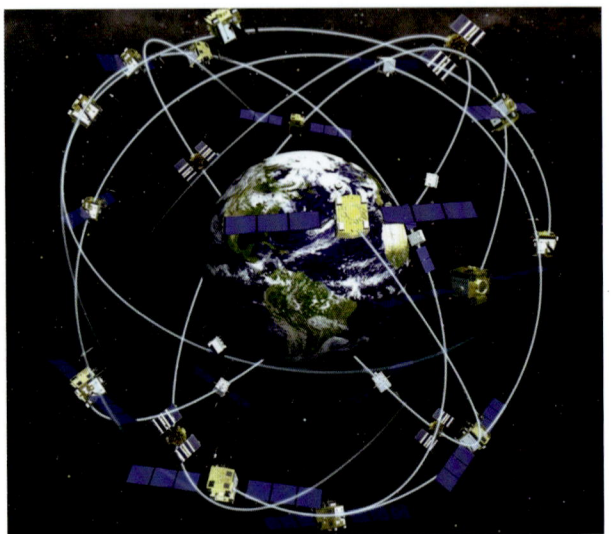

▲ Earth science satellites help NASA study the oceans, land, and atmosphere.

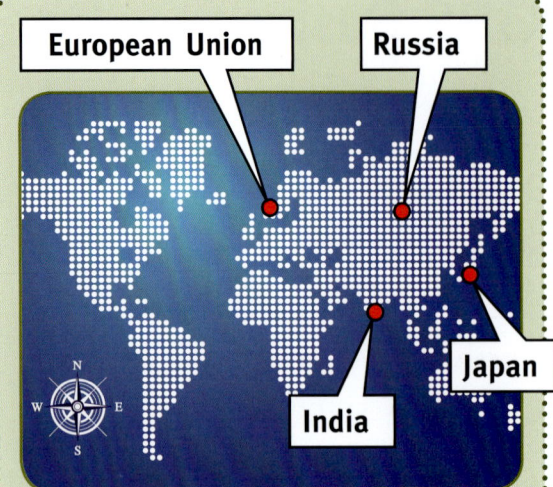

Satellite Systems Around the World

The United States was the first country to introduce GPS satellite technology. That was in 1974. Since then, other countries have introduced their own global positioning systems.

Japan: has satellites that orbit Japan and other areas of Asia

Russia: system similar to the GPS; twenty-four satellites orbit in three areas

India: system is much smaller version of the GPS

European Union: navigation system not expected to be fully working until 2020

How does GPS help scientists? What details in the text explain this?

6

How GPS Works

A group of kids are having a party and they want to order pizza—fast! But where is the nearest pizzeria? To find out, one of the girls types "pizza" into her smartphone. It brings up the names of local pizza places.

The smartphone was "smart"! It was able to know what particular pizzerias were near the party. The smartphone even knew its own location. This was possible because of GPS technology.

The Global Positioning System (GPS) is made up of satellites, ground stations, and receivers.

A Brief History of Navigation

Thousands of years ago people used landmarks, such as trees, to relay directions. In the Pacific Islands, some people made maps on clay tablets. Others used sticks and shells.

According to *National Geographic*, people native to the Pacific Marshall Islands used parts of palm tree leaves to show wave patterns between islands.

NAVIGATION TOOLS USED IN PAST CENTURIES

Tool	What It Was	When It Was Used	What It Did	What It Looked Like
Mariner's Compass	Early form of magnetic compass	From the Middle Ages (401 to 1500)	Indicated what course a ship is on in relation to north	
Nautical Charts	Early maps	Beginning around 1250	Not very accurate; no latitude or longitude labeled on maps	
Mariner's Astrolabe	An instrument for measuring angles of slope (or tilt) and elevation of an object	First used in the 1400s but goes back to ancient Greece	Used to determine the latitude of a ship at sea	
Sextant	Navigational instrument used to measure the angle between two objects	1501 to 1600	Measured the angle of stars, sun, moon; helped to determine longitude	
Chronometer	An instrument that could keep very accurate time	1761	Also used to determine longitude	

Records dating back as far as 3500 BCE show that sailors sailed close to shore so they wouldn't get lost. Eventually, they started using stars and planets for directions.

Finally, beginning in the twentieth century, scientists invented radio-based navigation. This system was able to locate objects by projecting radio waves against them. The ideas behind this system are still used today in GPS.

> What tool was first used in the 1400s? What details in the chart on page 8 explain what it was used for?

Latitude and Longitude

Latitude and longitude are two of the most basic and important terms in geography. Together, they describe the exact location of any place on the globe.

Latitudes are imaginary horizontal, parallel lines around the globe. They are 111 km (69 mi) apart. The most important line of latitude is the equator. It runs horizontally around the fattest part of Earth. Latitude describes a location's distance north or south from the equator.

Longitudes are imaginary lines that run vertically from the North Pole to the South Pole. The most important longitude line is the prime meridian. Longitude provides a way of telling how far east or west an object or location is.

Latitude and longitude lines are numbered. Every single place on Earth can be identified by where latitude and longitude lines cross.

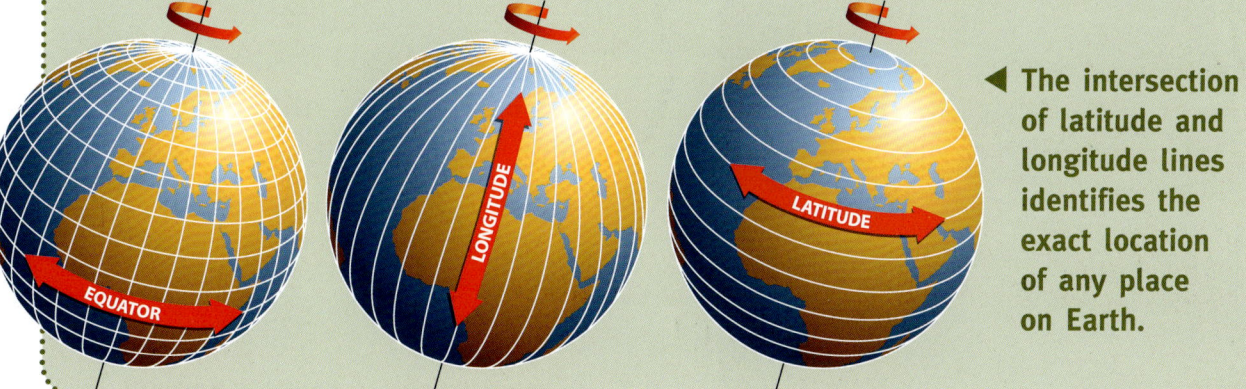

◀ The intersection of latitude and longitude lines identifies the exact location of any place on Earth.

The Development of GPS

In 1957, Russia launched Sputnik, the very first spacecraft, into space. Soon afterward, researchers at the Massachusetts Institute of Technology (MIT) discovered that the frequency of the radio signals sent out by Sputnik increased as the spacecraft got closer to their location. But they decreased as Sputnik moved away from them.

This discovery told researchers something they didn't know. A specific location on Earth could be determined using radio signals from a satellite. That was the first step in the development of GPS.

In the early 1970s, a scientist named Brad Parkinson got together with other scientists. They put together the details of the navigation system that would change the world.

They presented their plan to the U.S. military. And in 1978, the Department of Defense (DOD) launched the first working GPS satellite. It was called the Navigation System with Timing and Ranging, or NAVSTAR.

By the mid-1990s, the system was fully working with twenty-four satellites. It had become known simply as GPS. During these early years, the general public was not allowed to use GPS. That would all soon change.

◀ **This image shows a copy of Sputnik.**

Perfect Timing

Imagine a watch that gives nearly perfect time and costs $100,000! That is exactly what an atomic clock is. It is a special kind of clock that is both expensive and accurate.

All GPS satellites contain an atomic clock. GPS receivers on the ground match their time to these clocks.

"Time is critical to GPS," says Brad Parkinson.

"Locating a GPS receiver on the ground requires two main pieces of information," Parkinson explains. "First, you need to know the exact position of at least three satellites. Then you need to know the precise time a signal was sent out from each satellite. You use that information to calculate the distance from each satellite to the receiver. That tells you the receiver's position."

A GPS receiver can determine the current time within one-billionth of a second. That's because an atomic clock is so accurate it will lose or gain only one second every 300 million years!

▲ NASA is testing this new atomic clock for future deep space missions.

GPS: GUIDING THE WORLD

GPS was originally developed for the military. Today, it is used by people everywhere.

GPS Goes Mainstream

Over the years, many people have been involved in the development of GPS. Yet, there is one person who stands out for having the biggest impact on the future of GPS for the general public. That person was the fortieth president of the United States, Ronald Reagan.

In 1983, the Cold War[2] between the United States and the Soviet Union was at its height. Until then, the U.S. had allowed only the military to use GPS technology.

▲ Navigational GPS units like this are often used in cars to tell people how to get to places.

2. Cold War—a period of time following the end of World War II in 1945 in which there was political and military tension between the U.S. (and its allies) and the Soviet Union (and its allies)

12

The Fathers of GPS

Who was the father of the GPS? Actually, that title goes to three men.

Ivan A. Getting:
In 1960, Getting had the idea that satellites could improve navigation systems. Under his direction, scientists studied the use of satellites as the basis for a navigation system.

Roger Lee Easton:
In 1970, Easton developed an idea for a time-based navigational system. Also, he came up with the idea of putting atomic clocks in satellites.

Bradford Parkinson:
In 1973, Parkinson led the development of the first GPS, called NAVSTAR. What does he think about GPS today? "It's a gift to humanity," he says. "I'm really proud to say I had a small part in the beginning."

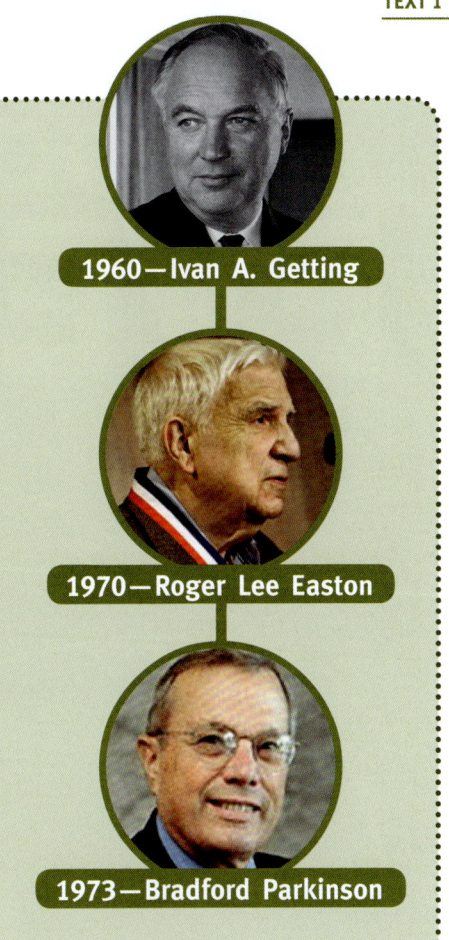

1960—Ivan A. Getting

1970—Roger Lee Easton

1973—Bradford Parkinson

President Reagan was concerned about American aircraft. What would happen if an aircraft's navigation system failed? What if it went off course and into the Soviet Union's airspace? In fact, that did happen when a Korean plane became lost over Soviet territory. That's when President Reagan opened GPS to civilians, or people not serving in the military. He hoped that it would help prevent something like that from happening again.

Soon afterward, scientists, private businesses, and individuals started developing ways to use GPS. At first, it was used mainly on passenger airplanes and boats. But soon many other uses for GPS emerged.

Today, GPS receivers are everywhere—from cars to smartphones.

What was happening in 1983? What details in the text explain how this was related to today's GPS use?

TEXT 2

A Tool for EVERYONE

From Navigation to Disaster Response

GPS has become part of almost everyone's life in one way or another. Here are some of the ways people use GPS today:

- Scientists use it to track the movements and feeding habits of animals they are studying.
- Online stores use GPS to track deliveries across town or across the world.
- Archaeologists use GPS while hunting for shipwrecks.
- Emergency teams use GPS to locate and rescue people faster.
- Parents use GPS to keep track of their kids in a shopping mall or amusement park.
- People of all ages use GPS for fun, such as in the treasure hunt activity called **geocaching**.

Undoubtedly, people will continue to discover new and beneficial uses for GPS in the future.

Mapping the World

People have used maps for thousands of years. In fact, one of the world's oldest maps was found on a stone tablet in Spain. It was nearly 14,000 years old! Over the years, mapmakers, called cartographers, drew maps.

Mapmakers today still draw maps, but they also use GPS technology to create them. Thanks to GPS technology, almost the entire surface of Earth has been mapped—from mountains and rivers to country roads and city streets. Using GPS to map an area has many advantages. Mainly, it saves time and money. Today, as *National Geographic* points out, "many people navigate using GPS units that communicate with satellites to determine their exact location on Earth."

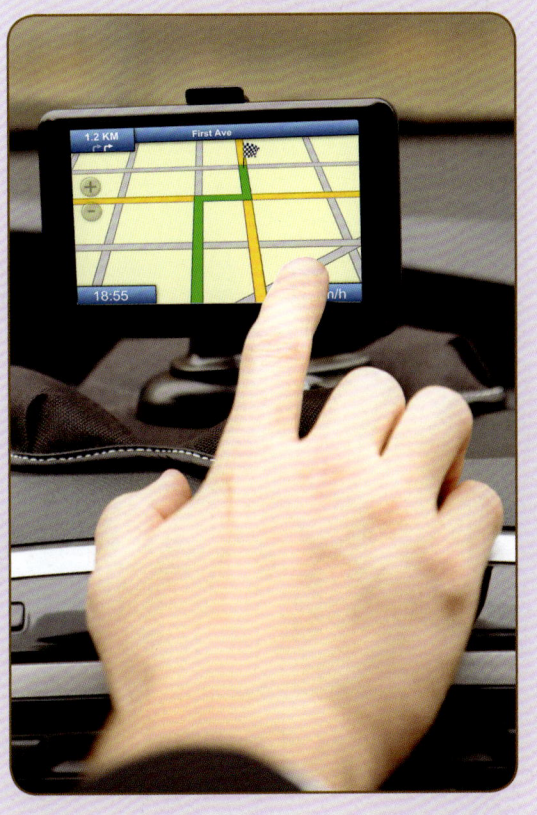

A TOOL FOR EVERYONE

"Search" and Rescue

Imagine this: A young woman decides to go for a hike in a remote part of the Grand Canyon. Suddenly, she is lost. What can she do?

Fortunately, this young hiker has an important device with her. It is a small, handheld satellite tracking device, called a **personal beacon locator (PBL)**.

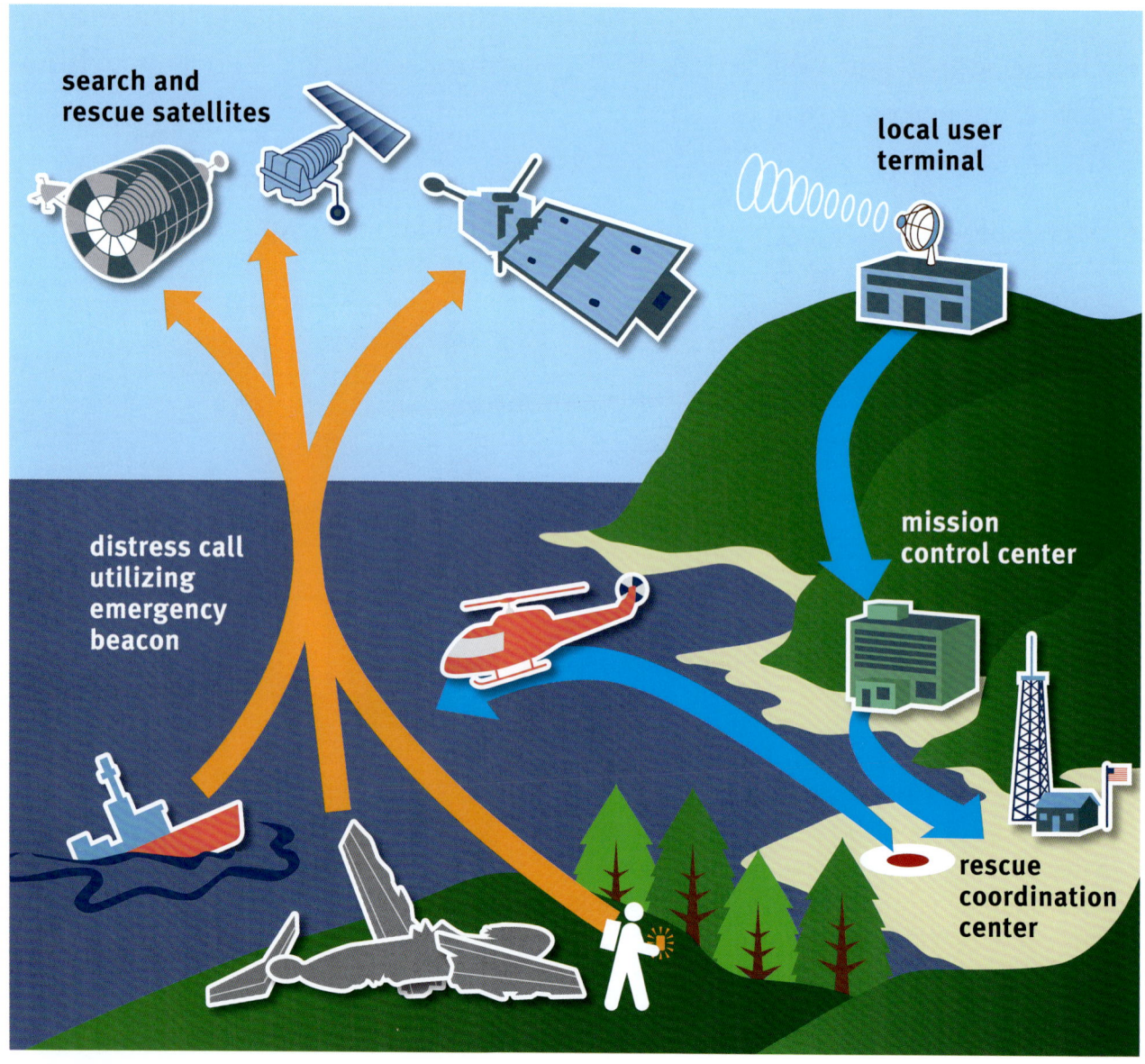

▲ Different types of satellites detect boats, aircraft, and people in distress. They send signals to ground stations where rescue teams are sent to help those in need.

16

▲ Abby Sunderland waves from her sailboat *Wild Eyes* before attempting to become the youngest person to sail solo around the world.

She pulls the PBL out of her backpack and presses a button. The PBL sends out an emergency signal. The signal is received by a weather satellite. It is then sent to a mission control station, which calculates where the distress signal came from. Finally, the control station sends the information to a rescue team.

This is all part of the Search and Rescue Satellite Aided Tracking System, or SARSAT. This system uses satellites to locate people in distress. During the past decade, SARSAT has rescued hundreds of people.

Rescue at Sea

In 2010, sixteen-year-old Abby Sunderland wanted to sail solo around the world.

Yet, on her journey, her forty-foot sailboat, *Wild Eyes,* ran into trouble. There were heavy seas that broke the main mast on her boat. Suddenly, she was faced with an emergency.

Fortunately, Abby had two PBL devices with her. She activated the devices, which sent out signals to orbiting satellites.

An emergency rescue team pinpointed where Abby was located in the Indian Ocean. The next day a fishing boat was sent to her location. She was rescued . . . thanks to her PBL and GPS.

In 2015 alone, SARSAT rescued more than 200 people on land and at sea. This technology is truly taking the "search" out of "search and rescue."

A TOOL FOR EVERYONE

▲ A bear wears a GPS collar for a scientific study.

GPS for Science

For many visitors to Yosemite National Park in northern California, there is nothing scarier than a run-in with a bear! Bears at Yosemite often wander into campgrounds, usually looking for food.

But now the park has a new tool to keep the bears in check. It is a GPS collar. So far, wildlife biologists have put these collars on nine bears to track their movement. "We can locate the animal and get it out of the area," says Ryan Leahy, a biologist at the park.

Early Warning System with GPS

Today, scientists are testing a new early warning system to find out if earthquakes can be predicted. The system uses GPS and other sensors.

According to the Scripps Institute of Oceanography in California, the system can detect earth movements seconds before a large earthquake. It can also determine if the earthquake is likely to generate a tsunami.

Today, GPS technology is helping to predict other natural disasters, such as flash floods. An early warning system can help emergency services be better prepared. It can provide important information to the public (often on their smartphones). And it can possibly even save lives!

▲ GPS stations like this one have small sensors to help predict earthquakes.

Bears aren't the only animals that biologists are tracking with GPS. Recently, fifty big sharks were tagged with GPS devices. An organization called Ocearch now knows where these sharks are—on any given day, at any given time. When the sharks get close to shore, an alarm is sent to lifeguards, who can warn swimmers to get out of the water.

But there is another advantage to tracking sharks through GPS. It gives scientists important new information about the movement and behavior of sharks.

▲ Thanks to GPS technology, scientists now know more about sharks than ever before.

A TOOL FOR EVERYONE

GPS for Fun

People have discovered many fun and creative ways to use GPS. One is geocaching, a modern-day treasure hunt activity that families from all over the world are participating in.

Geocaching participants navigate to a specific GPS location and then attempt to find the geocache, or container, hidden at that location.

Inside the container, there is a logbook for geocachers to sign. It is fun to see who else has signed the logbook and where they're from. Often, there is also a "treasure" to take, but the rule is take one and leave one.

The Fost family in Pound Ridge, New York, are active geocachers. Edie Fost, her husband, and their children have been geocaching for more than three years.

20

Recently, Edie and her family took part in an interview about their experiences with geocaching. Here is part of that interview.

Q: What kind of GPS device do you use?

A: We mostly use the geocaching app on our smartphone. At home, we prepare for the adventure by checking out locations and levels of difficulty on the computer at the geocaching website.

Q: How hard is it to find a cache?

A: The caches are rated on size and difficulty on the website. I always search for relatively easy caches to find. But if they are too easy to find, it isn't that much fun. But most are not actually that easy.

Q: What is the most exciting cache you have ever found?

A: One cache we really liked was a pencil cache. It contained only pencils and you were asked to leave only pencils. We left a pencil with an image of a popular video game character. But we took a pencil from a famous Broadway musical.

Q: What advice do you have for someone new to geocaching?

A: Ideally, start with someone who has already found the cache you are looking for. Once you've found the first cache, everything starts to make sense.

Q: What one word would you use to describe a geocache adventure?

A: Fun!

Geocaches

Geocaches are everywhere. In fact, there are nearly three million active geocaches throughout the world. There are more than six million geocachers! They all use GPS technology to navigate their way from one location to another.

A Look at the Future

There are several new ideas and inventions that will be possible in the future with GPS technology. A driverless car is one of them.

GPS technology in the roof helps a driverless car to safely navigate the road.

The biggest advantage of the new driverless car is that it may actually help prevent accidents. For example, there is no driver to fall asleep on the road. Also, it will determine a safe speed to travel in any situation.

Here are a few other new developments being made possible through GPS.

GPS Tracking "Bullets": Recently, some police departments have started using GPS "bullets" in car chases. These sticky GPS devices attach to the car being chased. The police can then track the vehicle using GPS data.

GPS SmartSoles: People with Alzheimer's disease lose memory. These people can wander off and not remember how to get home. Now, a new pair of shoes with a built-in GPS tracking device tells where the shoes are—and where the person is.

Future GPS devices will be smaller and more accurate. They will also make navigation even easier. And, more than likely, they will be able to do a lot more than simply get a person from one point to another.

▲ The tracking device in the shoe sends a signal to a satellite. It is then relayed to a relative's smartphone or computer.

GLOSSARY

celestial navigation (seh-LES-chul na-vih-GAY-shun) *noun* the science of finding one's way by observing positions of heavenly bodies (page 4)

geocaching (JEE-oh-ka-shing) *noun* a modern-day treasure hunt activity based on GPS technology (page 15)

navigation (na-vih-GAY-shun) *noun* the practice of planning and controlling the course of something, such as a ship (page 4)

orbits (OR-bit) *noun* curved paths in which planes, satellites, and spacecraft revolve about other bodies *verb* revolves about another body in a curved path (page 6)

personal beacon locator (PBL) (PER-suh-nul BEE-kun LOH-kay-ter) *noun* a tracking device or transmitter used in finding people in distress (page 16)

satellites (SA-teh-lite) *noun* artificial (man-made) or natural bodies that revolve around other heavenly bodies (page 4)

technology (tek-NAH-luh-jee) *noun* the use of science and engineering to do practical things (page 4)

INDEX

atomic clock, 11, 13

celestial navigation, 4

Cold War, 12

compass, 8

device, 5, 13, 16–17, 19, 21

driverless car, 22

equator, 9

geocaching, 15, 20–21

latitude, 8–9

longitude, 8–9

NASA, 4, 6

navigation, 4–6, 8–10, 13, 15, 22

NAVSTAR, 10, 13

orbit, 5–6, 17

Parkinson, Brad, 10–11, 13

personal beacon locator (PBL), 16–17

prime meridian, 9

Reagan, Ronald, 12–13

satellite, 4, 6, 10–11, 15–17

Sputnik, 10

Sunderland, Abby, 17

technology, 4, 7, 22

23

ANSWER TEXT EVIDENCE QUESTIONS

Use text evidence from both texts to answer these questions:

1. Look back at the sidebar on page 13. What happened in 1973? What details in the text explain why this was important to future navigation?

2. What are the three main parts of GPS? What details explain how these parts make the system work?

3. Look at the chart on page 8. What navigation tool was used from 1501 to 1600? What was it used for?

4. Refer to the sidebar on page 17. How did a PBL device help Abby Sunderland?

5. What historical space event occurred in 1957? What details in the text explain how this was the driving force in the development of GPS?

6. According to *National Geographic*, how were palm trees used in early navigation?

7. Review the information in both texts to explain how GPS has helped at least three different groups of people.

8. Look back at the section on geocaching. How has GPS made this activity possible?

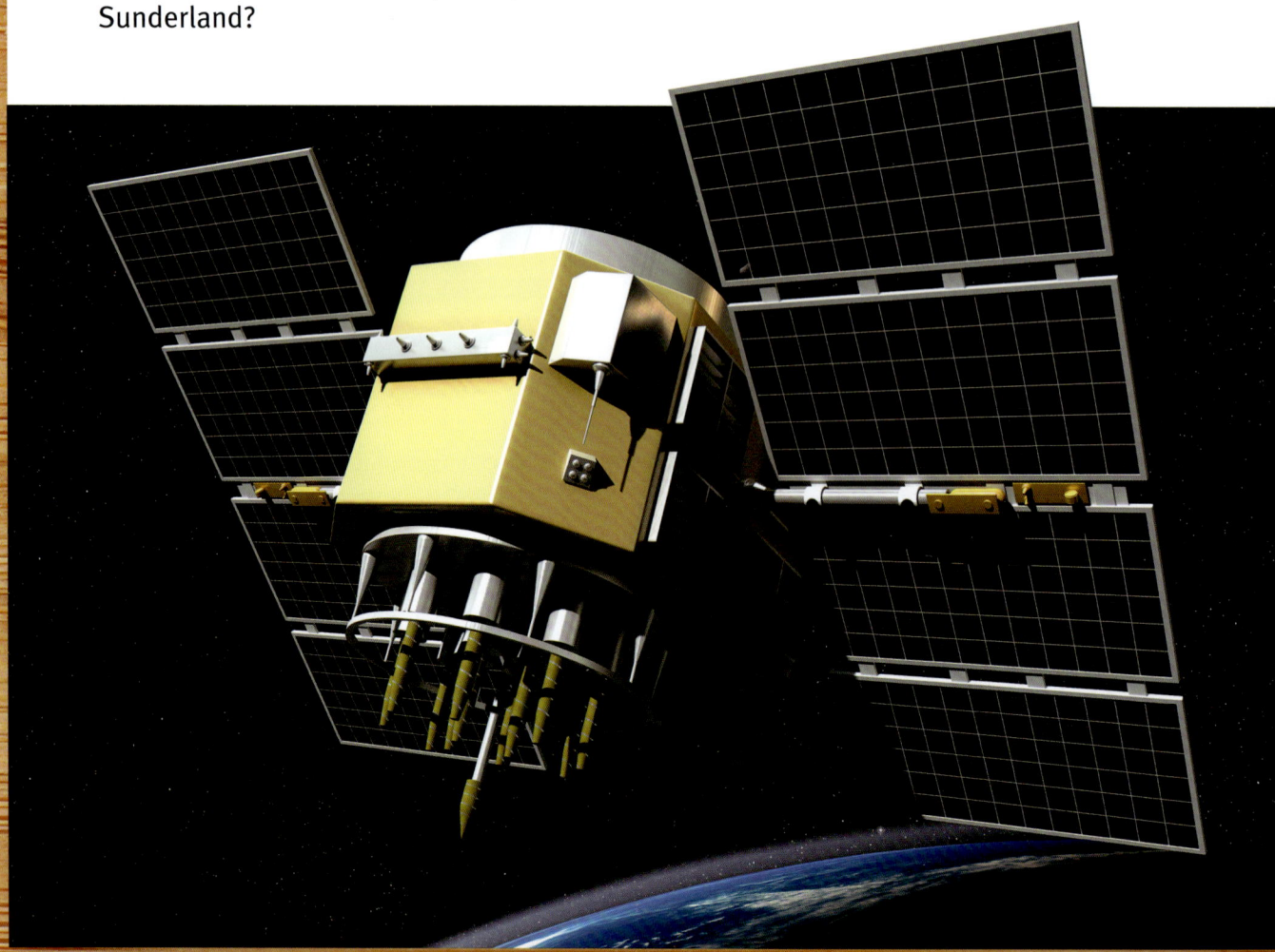

24